Tunnel Warfare

Fredonia Books
Amsterdam, The Netherlands

Tunnel Warfare

Adapted by Che Mei and Pi Lei

Illustrations by Chekiang Fine Arts Institute Drawing Group

ISBN: 1-4101-0738-8

Copyright © 2004 by Fredonia Books

Fredonia Books
Amsterdam, The Netherlands
http://www.fredoniabooks.com

All rights reserved, including the right to reproduce this book, or portions thereof, in any form.

SYNOPSIS

DURING China's War of Resistance Against Japan (1937-1945), the Japanese invaders in 1942 launched barbarous "mopping-up" campaigns against the Communist-led base areas in central Hopei Province. But the people there, every man, woman and child, inspired by Chairman Mao's thinking on people's war, joined in the war effort, closely co-ordinating with the Eighth Route Army units to develop guerrilla warfare over a large area, and creating the "tunnel warfare" that has become so well known. Making good use of tunnels, the army and people fought the Japanese aggressors and their local puppets, using various stratagems to wipe out the enemy's effectives. From an inferior force they grew into a strong one, going from the defensive over to the offensive at a time when the enemy was strong and we were weak. In the end the enemy "mopping-up" campaigns were smashed and the aggressors suffered decisive defeats.

Kao Chuan-pao

District Leader Chao   Kao Lao-chung

1. One early morning in 1942 the old bell sounds from a big locust tree in Kaochia Village, an anti-Japanese base in central Hopei Province.

2. Kao Lao-chung, village Party secretary, has got word that the Japanese at Black Gap gun tower are on the rampage again. He is telling the villagers to evacuate, and the militia to assemble.

3. Large, black clouds darken the sky as the enemy emerge to burn, kill and loot, devastating China's vast plains. This enrages the people.

4. To cover the evacuation, an Eighth Route Army unit under Company Commander Tsui keeps the enemy on the run while the villagers get to safety. Then the Army withdraws.

5. Hidden outside the village, the militiamen, who are eager to fight, are told by their militia commander, Kao Chuan-pao, to wait for orders. But Niu-wa is impatient and wants to join the regular troops.

6. Chuan-pao explains, "Don't look down on our militia! We're led by Chairman Mao and work closely with our regular force. If every village has its militia and guns, we'll drive out the Japanese invaders all right!"

7. Their discussion is interrupted by Party branch committee member Lin Hsia with a message for Chuan-pao: "District Leader Chao's come. He asks you to report at once."

8. "The Japanese around here have all hidden themselves in their 'tortoise shells' for the night," Chao tells Chuan-pao. Then he goes with Chuan-pao to look for the latter's father, Lao-chung, and tell him to assemble the militia and relay instructions.

9. Chao explains the situation and then reads out the district Party committee decisions: Mobilize the masses and rely on them, persist in the struggle till final victory. He takes out a red cloth-wrapped parcel, to which all eyes turn.

10. It is a copy of Chairman Mao's essay *On Protracted War*. This precious book heartens everyone.

11. "With the thinking of Chairman Mao, even if the sky falls we can find a way out!" says Lao-chung.

12. Lao-chung has studied Chairman Mao's teachings and learned much. He calls a Party branch committee meeting that night at which he says, "Comrades, in times of difficulty we must keep cool heads. Lin Hsia, will you read this for us?"

13. "To win victory, we must persevere in the War of Resistance, in the united front and in the protracted war. But all these are inseparable from the mobilization of the common people."

14. "Chairman Mao says that we must rely on the masses in whatever we do," Lao-chung sums up. "That way we'll certainly overcome any difficulty." Thus the Party branch decides to mobilize the masses to excavate for tunnel warfare.

15. Formerly each family had its separate cellar. Now the Party branch leads the village to build a tunnel network, linking every household.

16. While digging one day, Chuan-pao and his sister Mao-ni suddenly hear the sound of shovels, and immediately the tunnel is through. The comrades on both sides meet happily.

17. "Let's make it wider!" some suggest. But Chuan-pao says, "No, leave it. If the Japanese discover it and pump in water or gas, we can just fill it up. If they get in, we can deal with them here."

18. "Don't you think it'd be a good idea to conceal the openings?" Lao-chung adds. "Make them as inconspicuous as possible."

19. Niu-wa, impatient also with the digging, says, "How can we wipe out the enemy in their gun tower this way?" But Mao-ni tells Chuan-pao that the Young Women's Anti-Japanese Vanguard have assembled, and Lin Hsia asks him to review them.

20. With that Mao-ni is off like the wind, and Chuan-pao and Niu-wa see only Lin Hsia in the yard. She smiles when they ask where the others are. Suddenly the door opens and Mao-ni announces: "Here we are!" Then the door closes again.

21. Chuan-pao pushes the door open but sees no one. "Brother," Mao-ni calls again, "the opening is right in the room. Try and find it." He looks under the bench and beneath the mat but still can't find anybody.

22. Then Chuan-pao hears Mao-ni's voice again. He turns and sees her peeping out, smiling, from under the cauldron.

23. Chuan-pao is pleased and goes to the stove, but she is gone. Lifting the cauldron he hears from another direction, "Brother, we're here!" and looks out the door. The women are lining up in the yard.

24. Their leader, Su-yun, reports: "The Young Women's Anti-Japanese Vanguard are assembled and waiting for your instructions." Militia leader Chuan-pao is very glad, but doesn't know what to say.

25. Chuan-pao returns to the house, lifts the cauldron and jumps into the tunnel. Niu-wa follows him down.

26. Going some distance in the tunnel they come up through a feed trough. Lin Hsia admits proudly that it is their idea, while Niu-wa suddenly becomes enthusiastic about tunnel digging.

27. Traitor Tang Ping-hui, commander of the puppet troops at the gun tower, suggests a new attack on Kaochia Village. The Japanese captain Yamada adds, "The Eighth Route Army is too smart to be found in the daytime, we'd better attack at night. . . ."

28. Late that night Japanese and puppet troops surround Kaochia Village, and Yamada orders them to steal in.

29. The village is quiet under a new moon. Lao-chung, just back from the tunnels, hands the lamp to Mao-ni and says: "I'll go and inspect the sentries." She reminds him to hurry back.

30. In the pale moonlight, Lao-chung suddenly sees shadows moving about.

31. The enemy have entered the village! The villagers are unprepared. He must sound the alarm at once.

32. Lao-chung forgets all danger as he rushes to the old locust tree. Thinking only of the villagers' safety, he unties the clapper cord of the signal bell.

33. Suddenly he finds himself in a shaft of flashlight and, turning, sees the Japanese and their puppets in front of him.

34. Angry but undaunted, he sounds the alarm, which rings out in the night and terrifies the Japanese.

35. The people are alerted to the situation. Yamada, furious at being discovered, shoots twice at Lao-chung, wounding him. Still Lao-chung stands firm.

36. Lao-chung fearlessly takes out a hand-grenade and pulls the cord, ready to throw it at the enemy.

37. **"We the Chinese nation have the spirit to fight the enemy to the last drop of our blood."** With these words of Chairman Mao's on his lips, Kao Lao-chung hurls the hand-grenade. The enemy must not be allowed to have his way.

38. The hand-grenade kills several of the aggressors and their puppets. Kao Lao-chung dies heroically for his people.

39. From the sounds outside, the comrades who have withdrawn into the tunnel fear that Lao-chung has laid down his life. Hatred overcoming sorrow, Chuan-pao orders firmly: "Get ready to fight!"

40. Yamada and the traitor Tang can discover nobody and grumble: "We've got to find the door to their tunnel if we have to dig through the earth!" They tear down walls, wreck houses and gut the whole village.

41. Finally they discover a tunnel opening the villagers have not had time to cover, but, not daring to go in, they pump smoke into the tunnel.

42. As smoke fills the tunnel and the villagers start coughing, Lin Hsia and other militiawomen direct the villagers to seal off the opening with quilts.

43. The enemy find another opening and begin pouring bucketfuls of water into the tunnel.

44. Decisive action is needed. Chuan-pao calls Lin Hsia and Kang for a Party branch committee meeting. They decide to emerge through the stove opening and launch a surprise attack to engage the enemy while the villagers get to safety.

45. Everyone volunteers to be first, but Chuan-pao says he will. "You get ready to cover the villagers," he orders. Lin Hsia hands her pistol to Chuan-pao.

46. A couple of Japanese soldiers are humming a tune as they build up the fire to cook a chicken they've stolen.

47. In the tunnel beneath the stove, Chuan-pao guesses what is going on above. He swiftly slides the cover aside.

48. Pushing the cauldron up, splashing soup and all over the Japanese, Chuan-pao leaps from the hole and kills both of these enemy soldiers with a shot apiece.

49. Fighting his way out, Chuan-pao continues firing at the enemy. Then militiamen follow, and block the enemy in with him.

50. The villagers quickly emerge from under the cauldron and move to another tunnel.

51. With enemy bullets coming through the window, Chuan-pao organizes the militia to concentrate fire for a counter-attack while covering the mass evacuation.

52. Knowing that the enemy have attacked Kaochia Village this night, District Leader Chao calls the local detachment and the militia of every village in an emergency muster.

53. Chao says: "The enemy from Black Gap has surrounded Kaochia Village. We'll harass the enemy with 'sparrow' warfare and co-ordinate with the Kaochia Village militia."

54. The blowing of horns, popping of crackers and beating of drums outside the village makes it seem to the enemy as if our troops are everywhere.

55. The militiamen shoot from a sorghum field with shotguns they have made. These shots, sham mixed with genuine, make the enemy dizzy.

56. Yamada asks nervously who's doing the shooting outside the village. The traitor Tang replies in a quavering voice: "Imperial soldier, I'll tell you what. The Communist army is different from the Kuomintang. You can't tell who is soldier, who villager, no matter how clever you are."

57. The militiamen catch sight of the Japanese captain Yamada. Chuan-pao takes an avenging shot at him from the window.

58. It hits Yamada in the hip. He yelps and falls.

59. Yamada's puppets shoot at random for a while, then carry their groaning Japanese chief back to Black Gap.

60. Chuan-pao returns to the old locust tree where his father died. The sight of the devastated village prompts him to say to the district leader, "Old Chao, the enemy is running wild now, but he can't scare us. This blood debt must be paid with interest!"

61. District Leader Chao says: "We must listen to Chairman Mao, who asks us to temper ourselves in the forge of hard and bitter struggle." Before parting, he asks Chuan-pao to study Chairman Mao's essay *On Protracted War*.

62. Back home, Chuan-pao opens the red parcel left by his father and begins to read the book carefully.

63. "Destruction of the enemy is the primary object of war and self-preservation the secondary, because only by destroying the enemy in large numbers can one effectively preserve oneself."

64. He understands better as he reads, and calls the militiamen to study with him: "The object of self-preservation is to destroy the enemy, and to destroy the enemy is in turn the most effective means of self-preservation."

65. After reading from Chairman Mao's essay, Chuan-pao says: "If we think only of sheltering and not fighting we'll end up taking the blows. We'll have to make the enemy's rear area into their front and give them no peace." Chairman Mao's teaching raises the morale and confidence of all.

66. The district Party committee instructs that the tunnel must not be only a shelter; it must be proof against water, gas and penetration, be both a bunker and a shelter. Chuan-pao sketches a plan for improving the tunnels.

67. Lin Hsia and Kang still see a light in Chuan-pao's house at dawn, and go to discuss the plan with him.

68. After taking the plan to the masses and getting their suggestions, the Party branch leads the militiamen in starting to work.

69. The mass movement for improving tunnels starts, with every man, woman and child joining in the work.

70. When District Leader Chao comes to Kaochia Village, Chuan-pao shows him the sketch. "According to the instruction of the district Party committee we've prepared against any eventuality. Look. . . ."

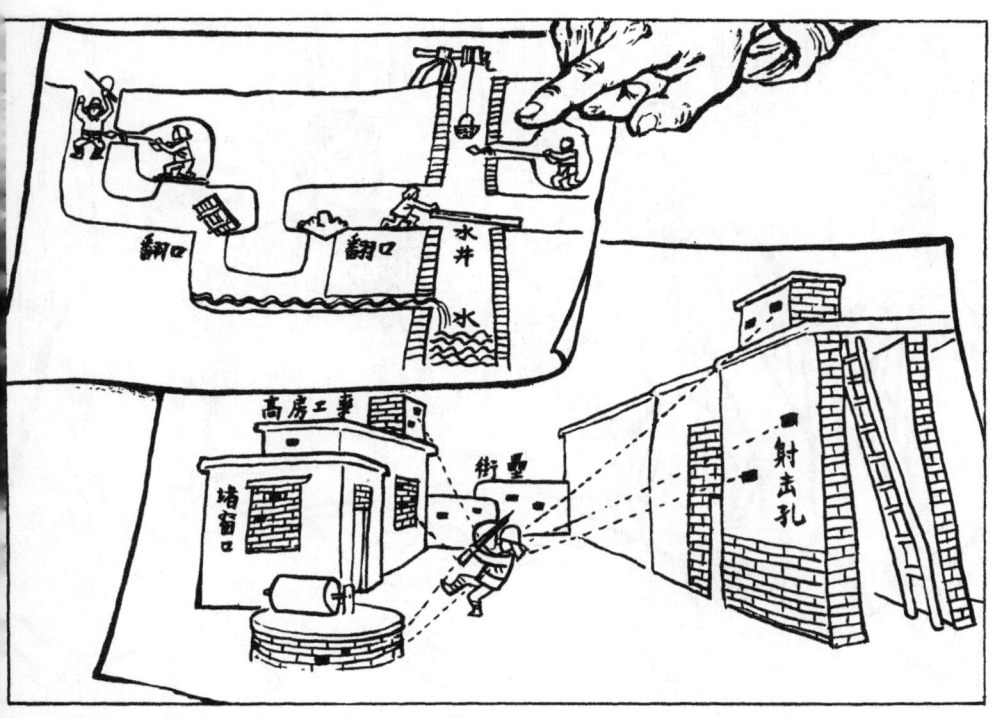

71. "This trap-door closes off fire, smoke and poison fumes. To the side of the entrance is a dug-out where one person with a stout spear can prevent the penetration of the enemy. Underneath is a drain to let off water. . . ."

72. District Leader Chao is pleased. "Very good, the tunnels have many advantages. Other villages should do this. And now for some good news: our military sub-region head is sending an armed work team here."

73. This news is eagerly received and, when the group arrives, Kang takes them to the village office.

74. Kang asks a few questions. Then the head of the group presents a letter of introduction. Seeing the red seal of the military sub-region on the letter, Kang asks them to take a rest while he goes to look for Chuan-pao.

75. As soon as Kang goes out, the men plot together. Their chief says: "Keep quiet and watch what I do. First, we've got to find out about their tunnels; then when Commander Tang comes, we'll get busy."

76. Kang soon returns with Chuan-pao, and when they are in the yard, one of the strangers quickly closes the door. Chuan-pao gives him a guarded glance, then proceeds calmly into the room.

77. Chuan-pao sizes these men up as he chats casually with them for a while. He feels that something's wrong.

78. Chuan-pao notices that some eggs that were on the table have disappeared and cornbread muffins are scattered all over the place. He thinks: "Our Army never wastes grain. These don't look like our men! Who are they anyway?"

79. The chief of the enemy agents takes out a fake tunnel sketch, saying: "Other villages have all made very fine tunnels." But when Chuan-pao reaches for the sketch, the man slyly draws it back. "How about visiting the tunnels in your village first?" he says.

80. Chuan-pao replies meaningfully: "As to the tunnels in our village, we have a network of them both inside the village and out. If the enemy dare to come, they'll never get back." The enemy agents shudder at these words.

81. Chuan-pao's suspicions are fully aroused. While passing a bowl of water to their chief, he picks up the rifle on the table. The man is alarmed and turns so quickly to seize the rifle that the bowl crashes to the floor.

82. Just then Su-yun hurries in to report: "Commander, a big Japanese detachment is coming!" The enemy agents, exposed now, do not conceal their satisfaction at this news.

83. Kang wants to assemble the militiamen but the enemy agent chief prevents him, asking him to show them into the tunnel. "We can't open fire!" Chuan-pao says. "There are a lot of enemy soldiers and so few of us. Let's all get into the tunnel." He squeezes Kang's arm so that he understands.

84. Removing the cover, Chuan-pao points to the entrance. "Please," he says. The agents peer down, a little afraid.

85. As Chuan-pao goes down into the tunnel the enemy agent chief forces him between two of them.

86. The enemy agents can see nothing in the pitch darkness of the tunnel, and have to obey Chuan-pao's orders. When Chuan-pao gets to the top of a tunnel ladder he kicks one, and knocks the other, to the bottom.

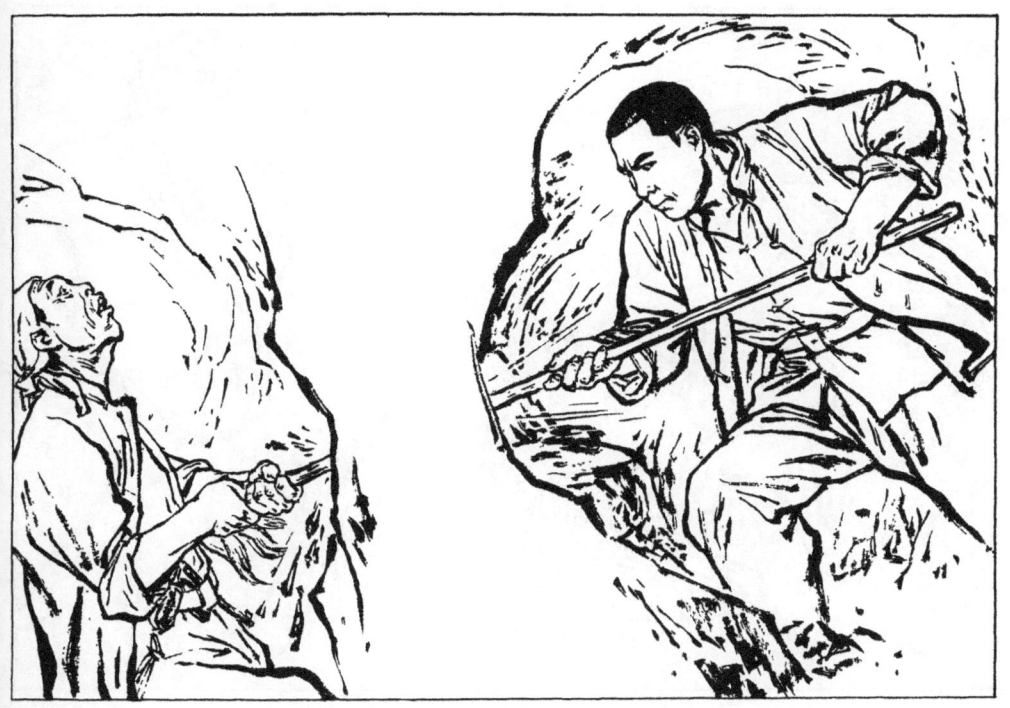

87. Chuan-pao closes a trap-door which separates the two. When one of the agents tries to get away, Chuan-pao slips into a side passage and plunges a red-tasselled spear into his heart.

88. The other enemy agent is looking for a way out when Chuan-pao calls. "Hey, you can't go that way! Come this way!" The agent takes only a few steps before he lands in a pit full of spikes.

89. After Chuan-pao has gone below with the two agents the rest get rough, and Kang and his militiamen take them on in hand-to-hand fighting. Just then Commander Tsui arrives with the real armed work team. "Don't make a move," he orders.

90. "Oh, this is a mistake," the enemy agent chief pleads. "We're sent by the district chief Chao." "Sun Chin-tsai, you impostor!" District Leader Chao comes in and exposes the enemy agent Sun, who falls to his knees shaking with fear.

91. Suddenly firing is heard, and the enemy agent chief Sun jumps up exclaiming, "Ha, ha, our troops have come and you're surrounded. Let me go quickly!"

92. Chao says: "Sun Chin-tsai, don't laugh too soon! Your 'troops' have been beaten off, and you're finished!" Chao tells the armed work team to tie up the agents and take them away. The district fighters arrive smiling, with rifles they have captured from the enemy.

93. Chuan-pao is ready to take on the other agents and comes out through a brick bed with a few militiamen. He sees District Leader Chao and Commander Tsui instead.

94. "Here's the real armed work team you long to see!" District Leader Chao introduces Commander Tsui to Chuan-pao, who shakes Tsui's hands excitedly. Chao says: "We must prepare. The Japanese are sure to retaliate."

95. Several days later word arrives that the Japanese are coming. The militia assemble at the sound of the bell. Chuan-pao says: "We'll divide up the work, follow orders and fight according to plan. We'll let the enemy in, but they won't get back."

96. A large force of Japanese and puppet soldiers steal towards Kaochia Village with rifles and cannons. But as they cross a bridge our militia fire on them, killing and wounding them and throwing them into confusion.

97. The furious Yamada desperately orders an artillery attack on Kaochia Village.

98. Chuan-pao orders the militia not to shoot. "Chairman Mao teaches us that if the enemy are strong and superior, and we are weak and inferior, we must use our advantages against their disadvantages. We'll lure the enemy into the village, where their guns will be useless and they'll be in our hands."

99. The firing stops, and the Japanese invaders slip into the village.

100. Once in the village the aggressors are like a wild bull in a ring of fire. As Chairman Mao says: **"The flexible employment of his [a commander] forces is the most important means of changing the situation as between the enemy and ourselves and of gaining the initiative."** Kao Chuan-pao and some militiamen dive into the tunnel to take their positions, watching the enemy carefully.

101. When the enemy enter the village, Chuan-pao shouts through a bamboo communications tube: "Attention every fighting group! Ready for independent combat. Change position after each shot. Make every bullet count."

102. The enemy draw to within 50 metres, the militia watching silently. Then the order "Fire!" is relayed throughout the tunnel complex.

103. Bullets fly at the enemy from everywhere. Kang is ordered to go with his machine-gun to fire from a height, and climbs between two walls.

104. Kang again shifts into a tree hollow and fires down on the enemy.

105. The battered Japanese run to the stone roller for shelter, but shots come from under it, picking off several more of them.

106. When the enemy scatter into our mined area a militiaman sets the mines off, and more enemy soldiers bite the dust.

107. Niu-wa discovers enemy soldiers approaching and emerges from the tunnel through the feed trough. He tosses hand-grenades, which explode among the enemy.

108. The militiamen get about freely from house to house and onto rooftops, from the yard into the tunnels. The Japanese are badly battered and can't go a step further.

109. Kaochia Village becomes a fighting citadel and every villager a soldier shooting at the enemy from all directions — from rooftops, trees, corners of walls, from behind houses, doorways, windows, the roadside and courtyards. The enemy are paralyzed.

110. The Japanese intruders are defeated. Kaochia Village resounds with laughter as the villagers collect the enemy guns and lead the captives off.

11. As the war develops the Kaochia Village militia, helped by the Eighth Route Army's armed work team, devises a wide network of tunnels linking with other villages, for offensive as well as defensive use.

112. The tunnel extends right up to the Japanese gun tower, so the militia can keep an eye on them or spring a surprise attack.

113. The Party Central Committee's call to expand the liberated area and shrink that held by the enemy, sparks a new attack on Black Gap. At a village cadres meeting Chao plans joint action of regular and local forces to capture Black Gap.

114. "First, we'll encircle Hsiping with the militia from ten villages," says Commander Tsui. "The county and district units will wait in the tunnel between the two strongpoints and lure the enemy out of their gun tower. Once the enemy leave their stronghold the district's regiment will capture Black Gap."

115. Nervous from the tunnel warfare, the Japanese captain Yamada listens everywhere for any sound of digging.

116. When Yamada receives a telegram from Hsiping requesting a relief force, he is worried. Pacing the floor and going to the map, he cries: "Attack Kaochia Village tonight!" Traitor Tang fawningly pronounces the plan "brilliant."

17. That night the enemy leave Black Gap and head for Kaochia Village.

118. News of the enemy's sneak attack on Kaochia Village soon reaches District Leader Chao and Chuan-pao. "We'll give them a hot reception!" says Chuan-pao. "No matter how many come, our militiawomen alone can handle them."

119. "If the enemy want to play tricks, we'll beat them at their own game and attack Black Gap," says Chao. "We'll smash their stronghold, catch and destroy them outside their lair," replies Commander Tsui confidently.

120. Niu-wa reports to Lin Hsia and other village women that the Japanese will sneak up on the village that night, that they should prepare for battle.

121. That night at Kaochia Village the traitor Tang is very cocky after discovering a tunnel entrance. "Go down and see if anyone's there," he says to two puppets.

122. The hole is a **booby-trap set for** the enemy, and the two puppets are soon taken captive. On Su-yun's order a puppet shouts out to the others: "The villagers are all in here! The imperial soldiers will have to come down or we can't get them out!"

123. Japanese soldiers go down and Su-yun closes the gate. The militiawomen fire through the tunnel wall and kill them all. There were twelve.

124. The Japanese second lieutenant goes down; then scared by a mine hanging overhead, he steps back into a death trap.

125. When nobody comes up, Yamada and the traitor Tang guess something's wrong and order the puppets to pump water into the hole.

126. But the precious water is returned back into the well and the enemy's plot fails.

127. The enemy try poison gas next, but the tunnel is blocked and the gas belches back outside.

128. The Japanese invaders' tricks have all failed and now it is our turn. The militia-women fire from different directions, pinning down the enemy.

129. Enemy remnants who rush into the houses are killed one after another by militia waiting for them.

130. Eighth Route Army fighters and militia under Commander Tsui rush towards Black Gap by tunnel.

131. Our Army, local detachments and militia join forces and advance on the Black Gap enemy gun tower.

132. The enemy gun tower is in view. At sight of this enemy strongpoint on China's plain where the Japanese fascists have slaughtered so many people, our fighters can hardly wait to demolish it.

133. Spearhead fighters charge ahead and knock out the enemy guards, while others rush up with dynamite.

134. The gun tower at Black Gap is blown to pieces, with bricks flying, flames and smoke leaping. The fighters charge into the fort.

135. To deal with the enemy fleeing from Kaochia Village back to their Black Gap, Chuan-pao leads the militiamen quickly and skilfully to lay a minefield.

136. Another mighty burst of dynamite and the enemy gun tower is blown sky high. Chuan-pao orders the militiamen to get ready to strike at any enemy that tries to escape.

137. Shattered and demoralized with their gun tower gone, the enemy run for their lives. But they run into the deadly blows of our militia, or step on mines, while those on horses are thrown off.

138. A bugle gives the signal for our men to pursue the enemy.

139. Thousands of our fighters appear on the plain as if from nowhere.

140. A fierce battle rages as the people, with the tunnel warfare they have created, plunge the Japanese invaders and their puppets into a sea of people's war.